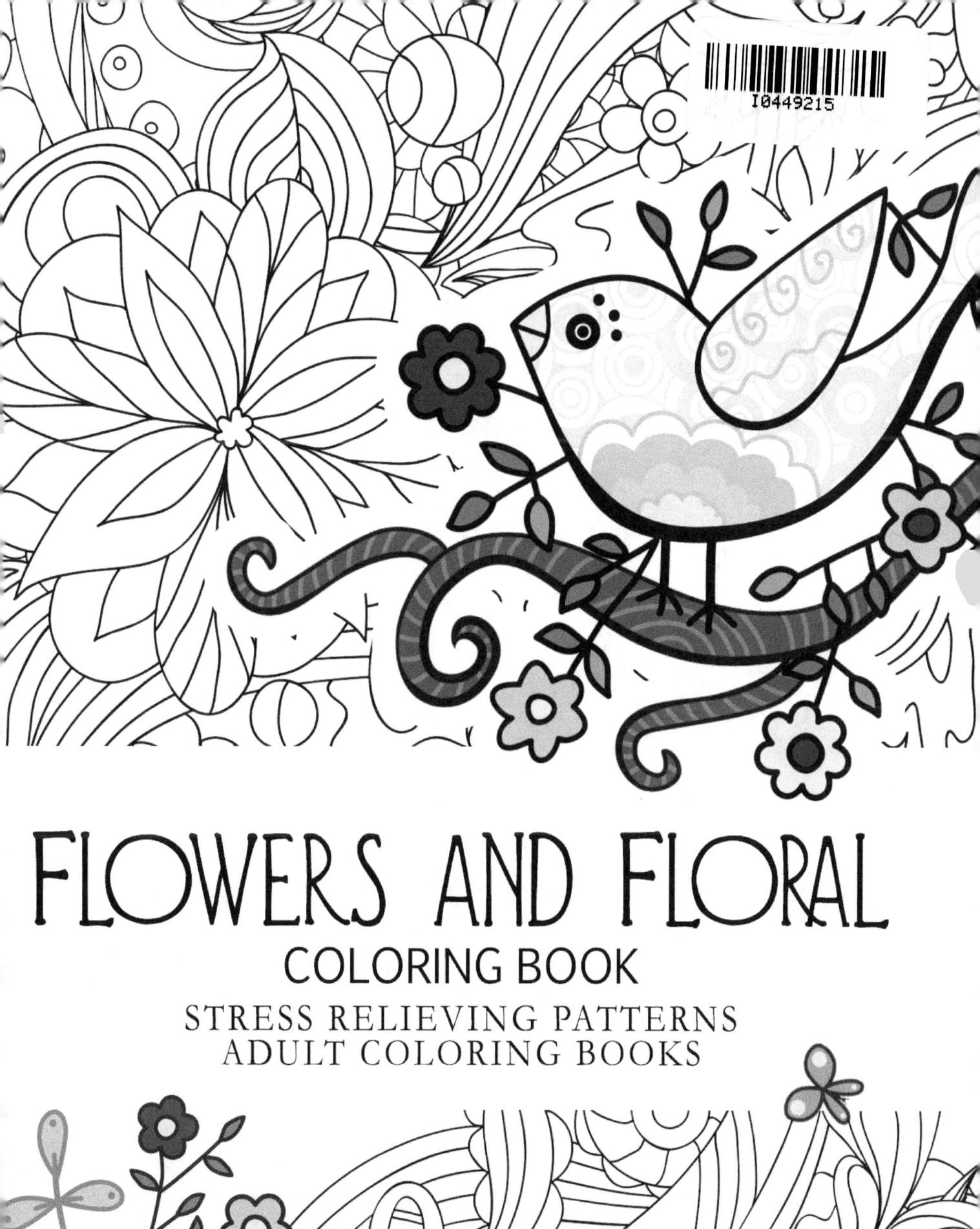

FLOWERS AND FLORAL

COLORING BOOK

STRESS RELIEVING PATTERNS
ADULT COLORING BOOKS

COLOR TEST PAGE

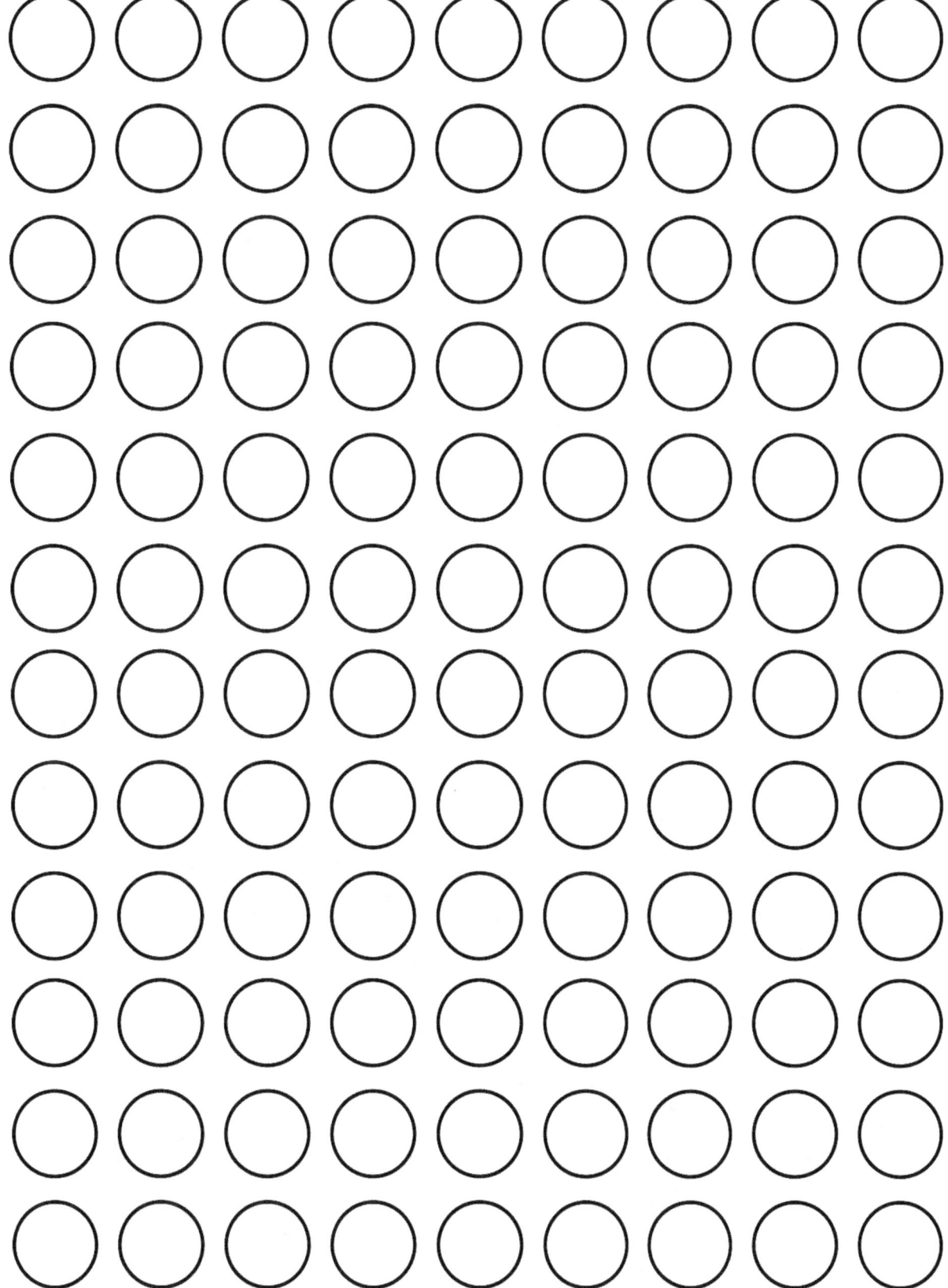

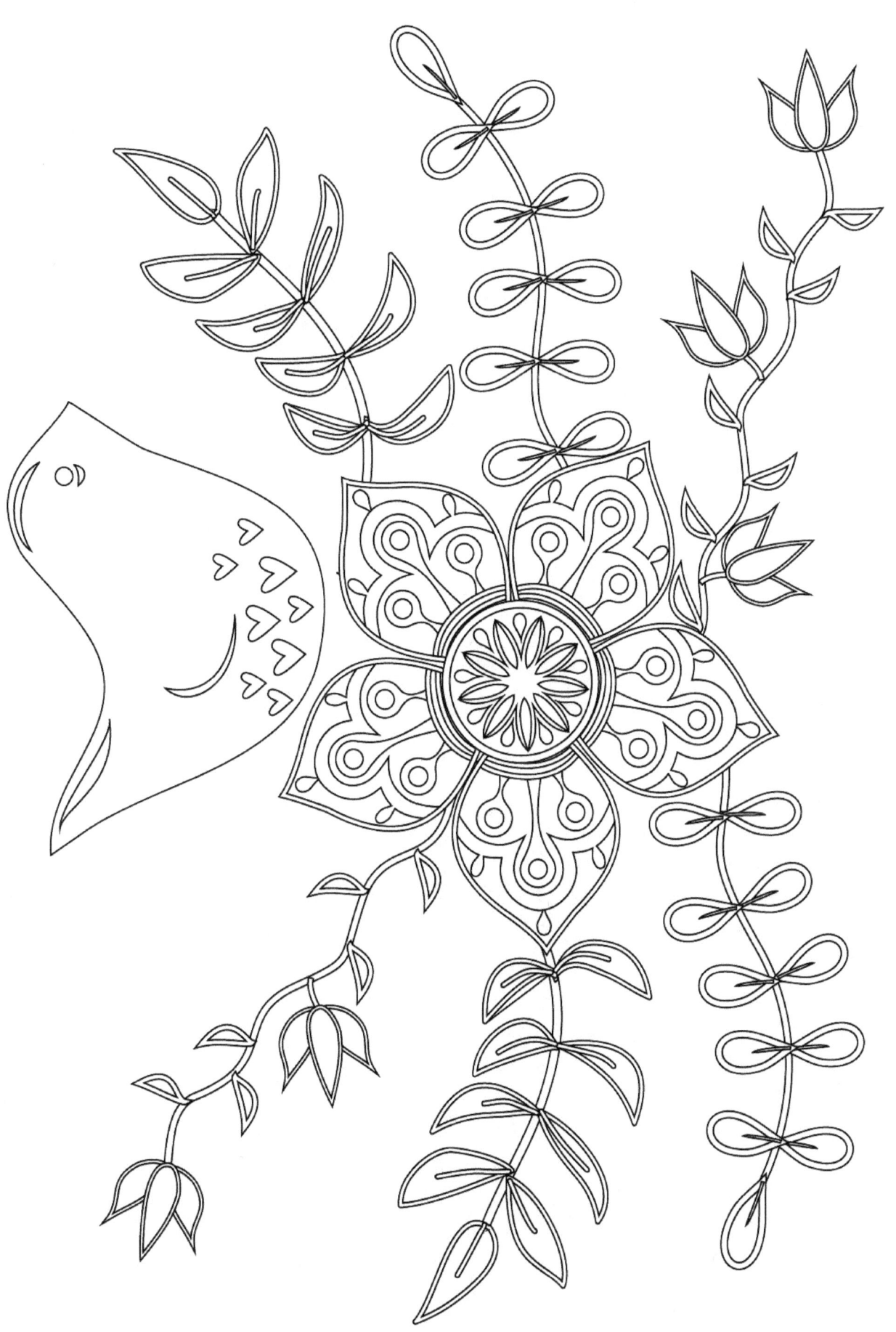

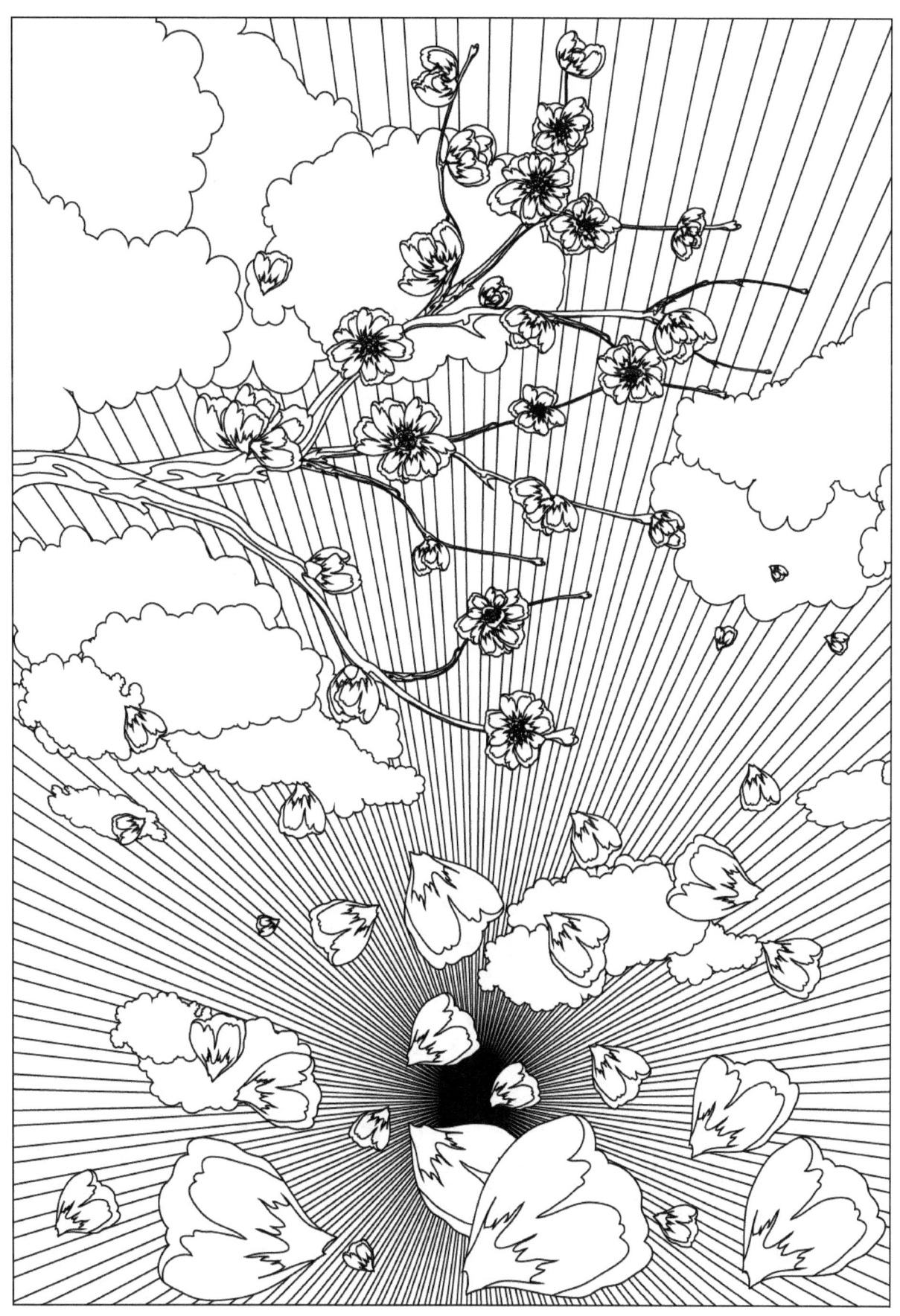

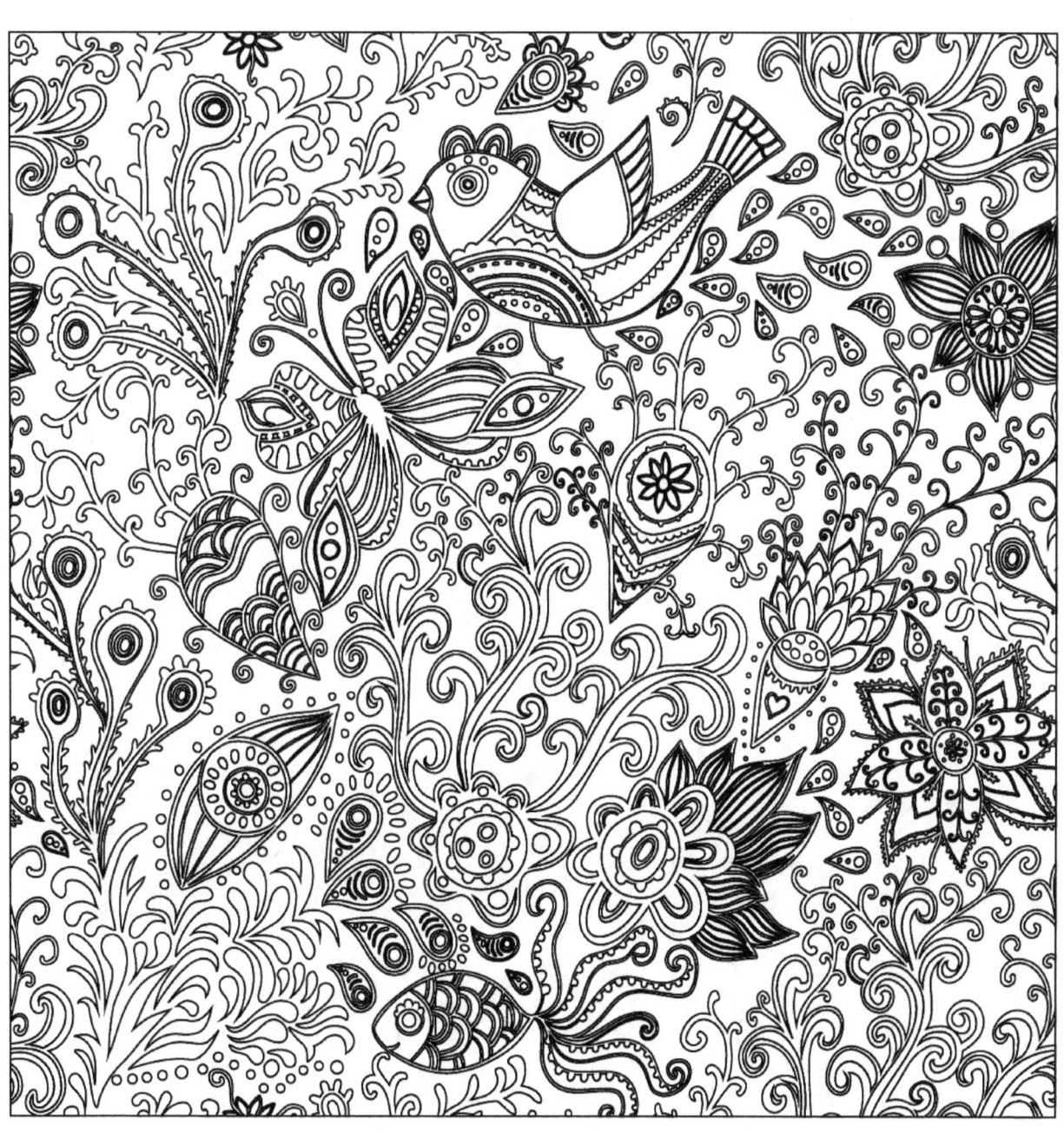

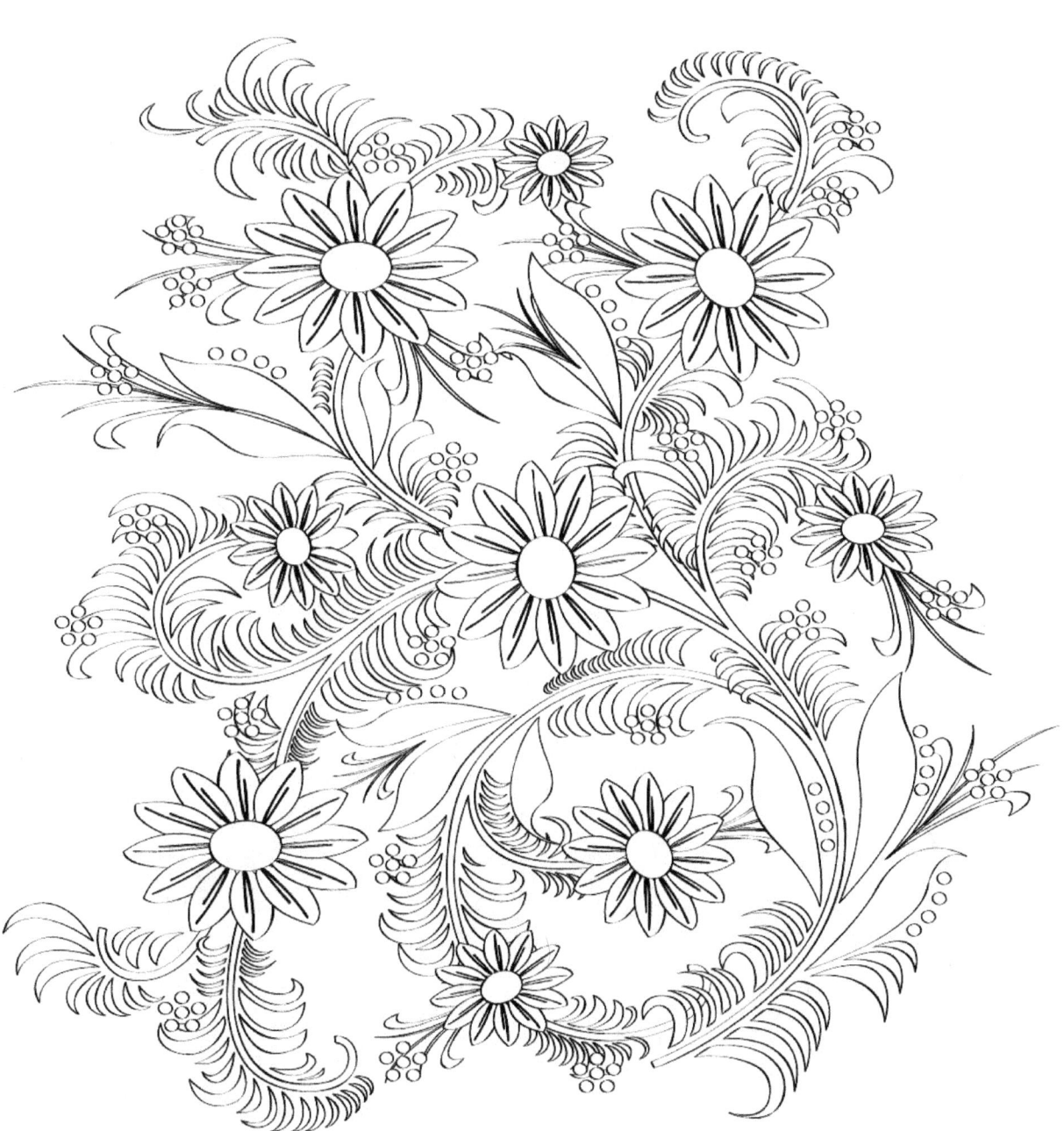

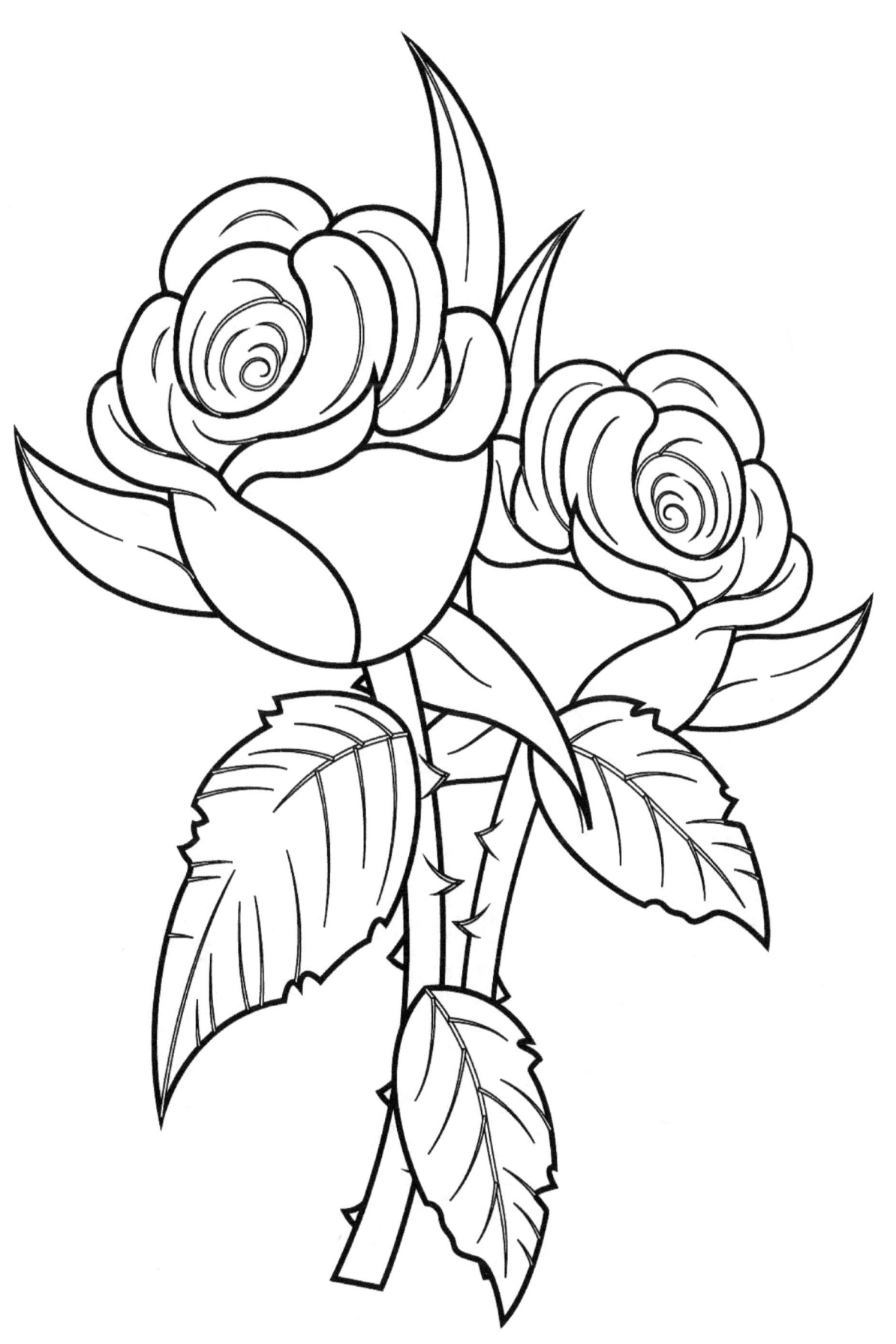

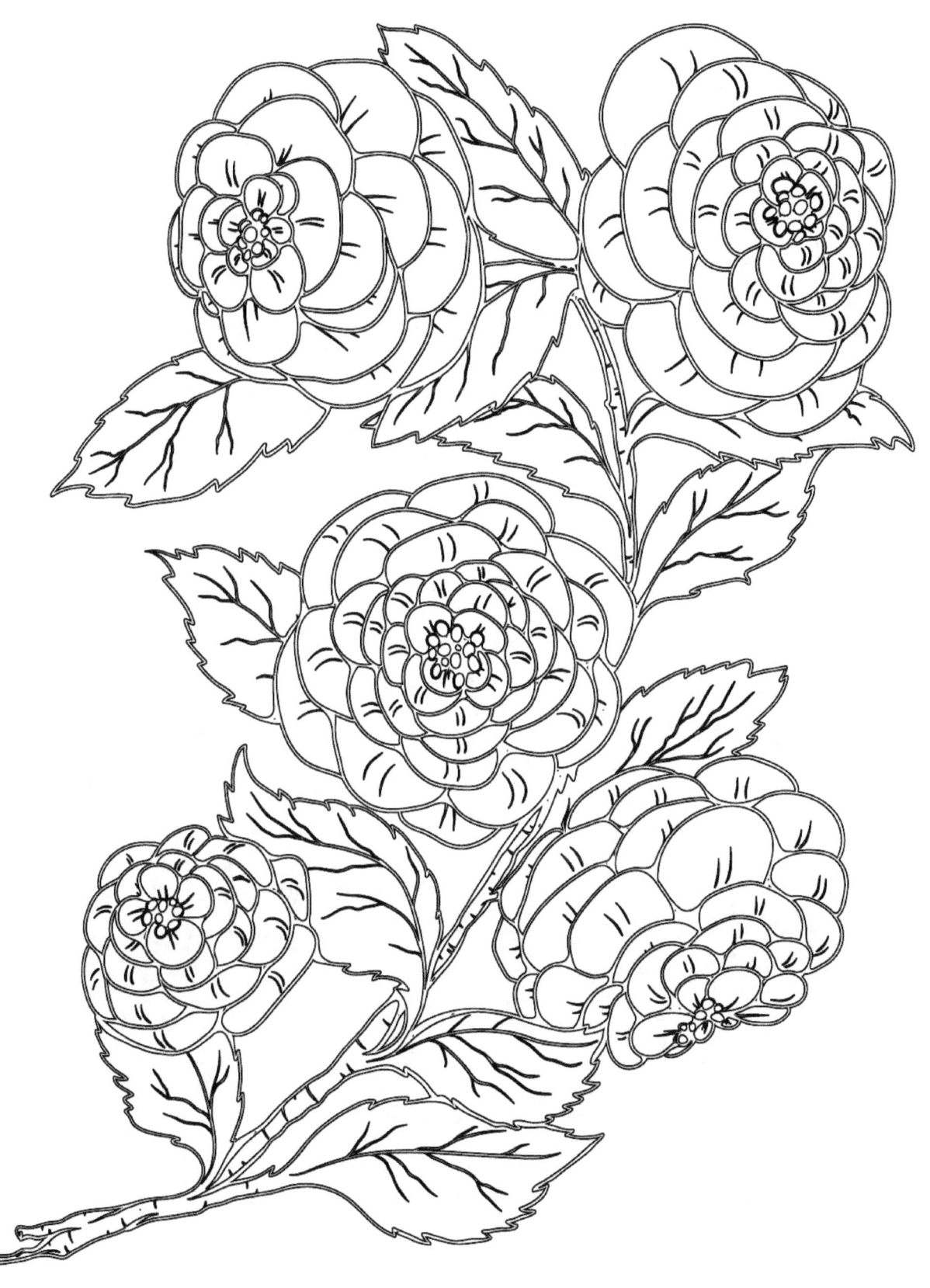

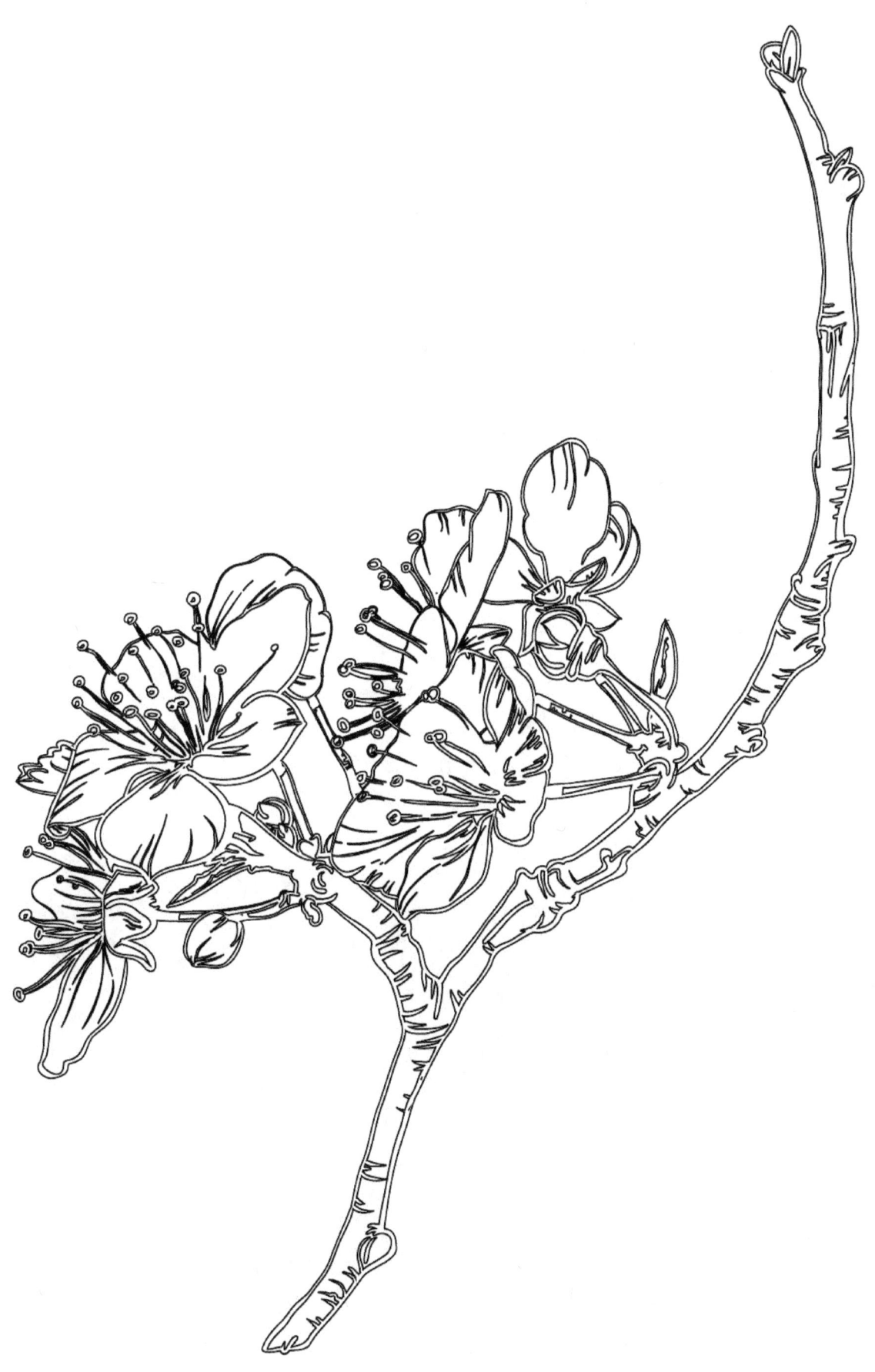

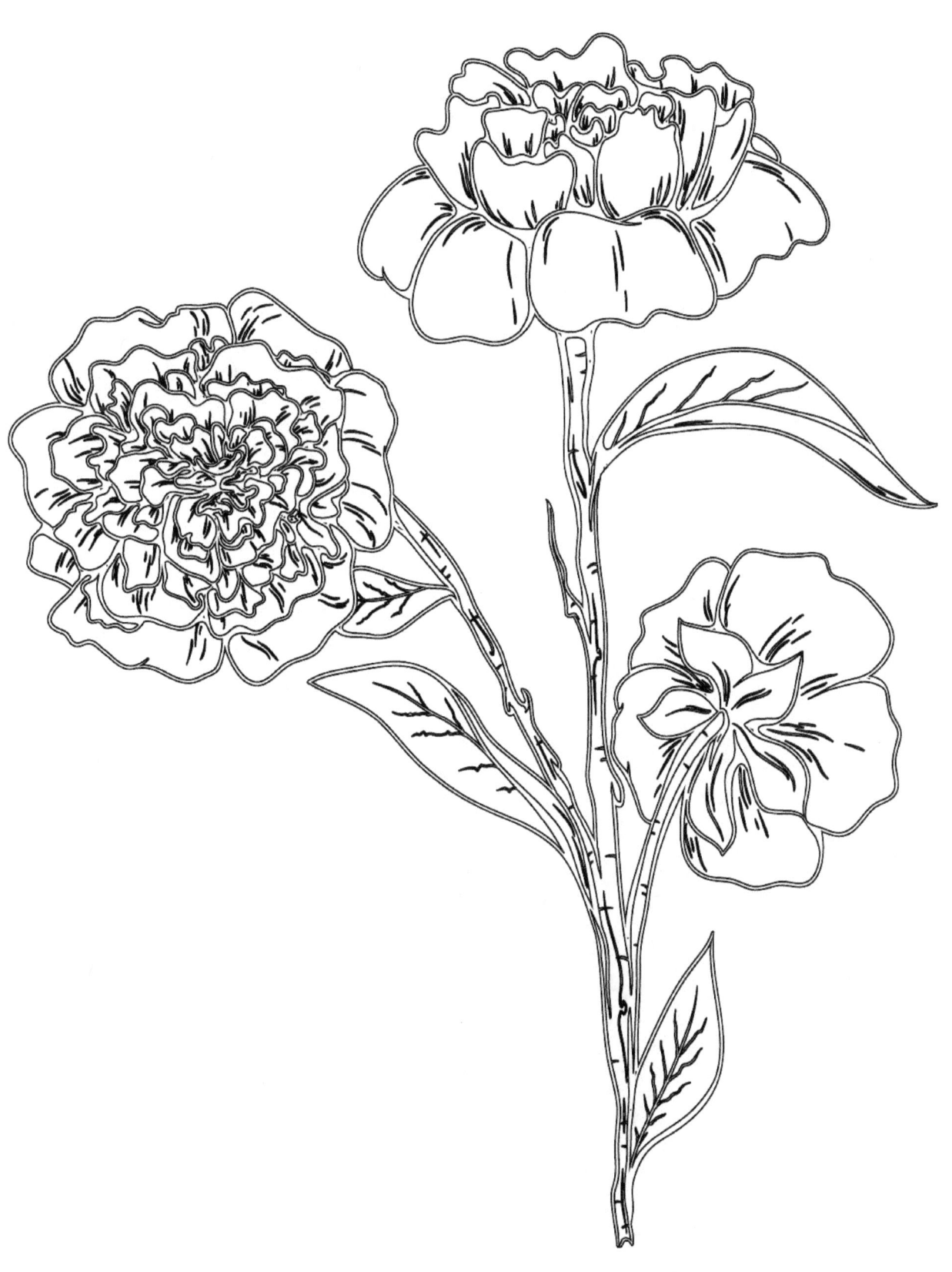

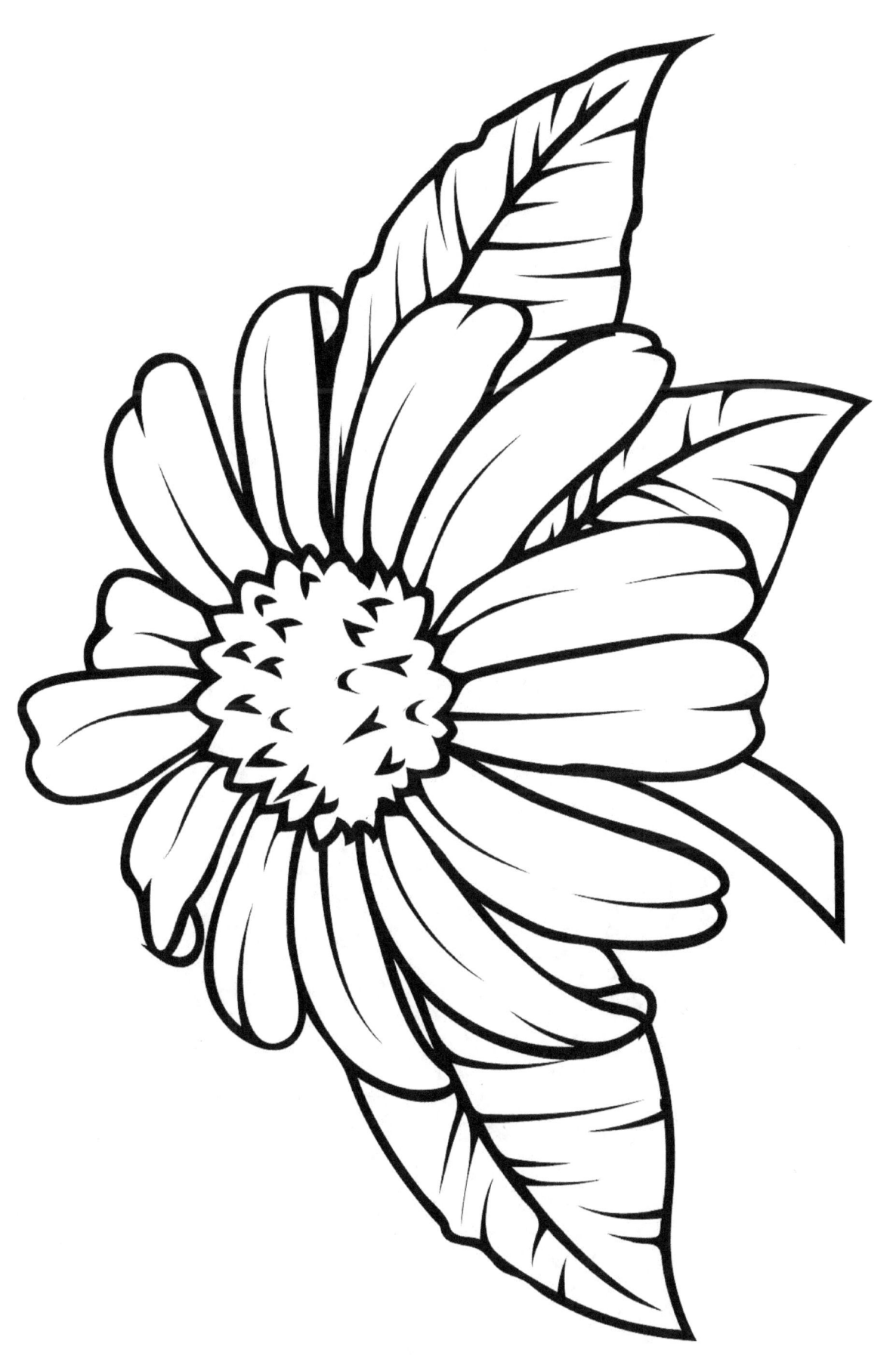

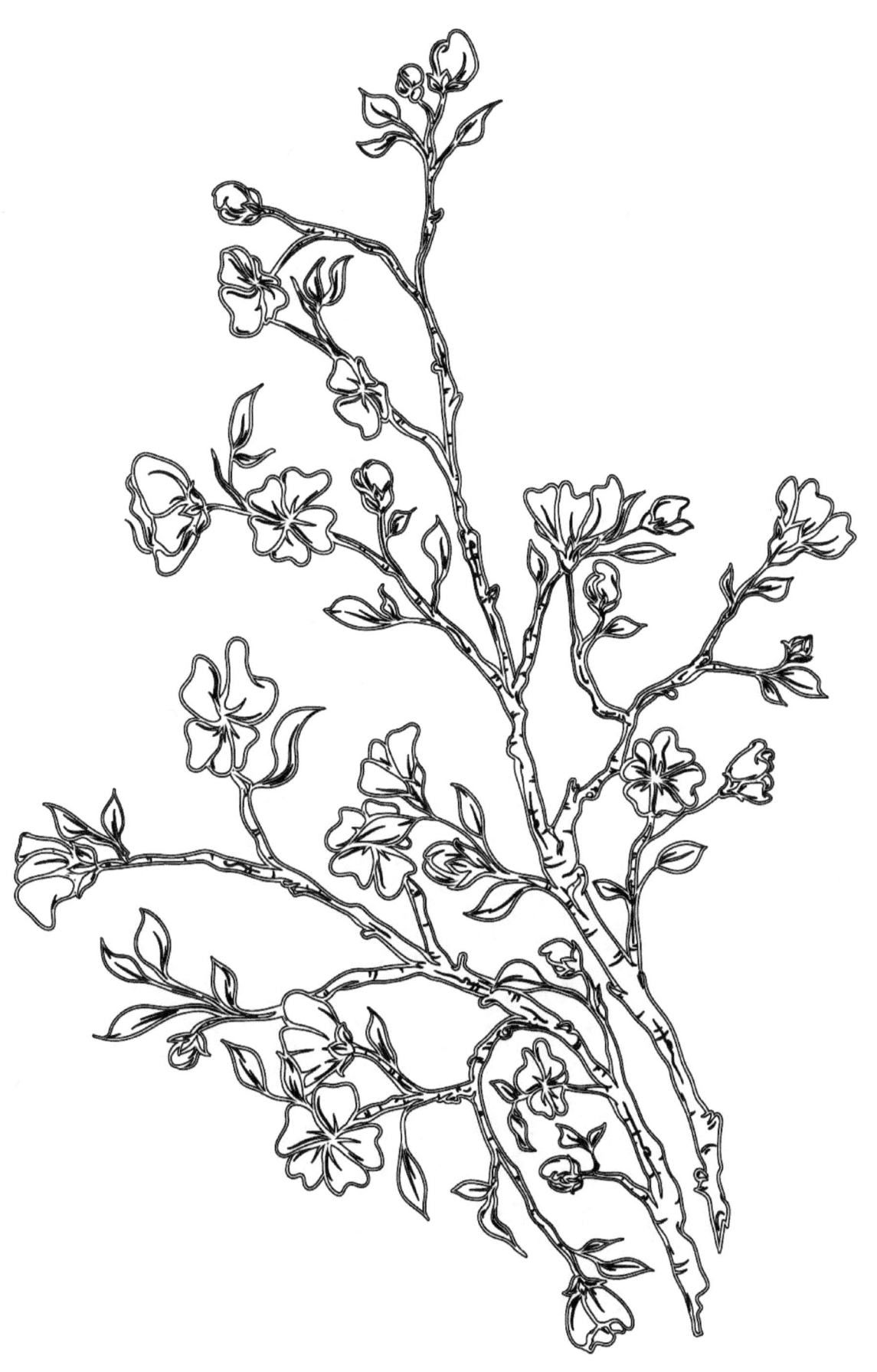

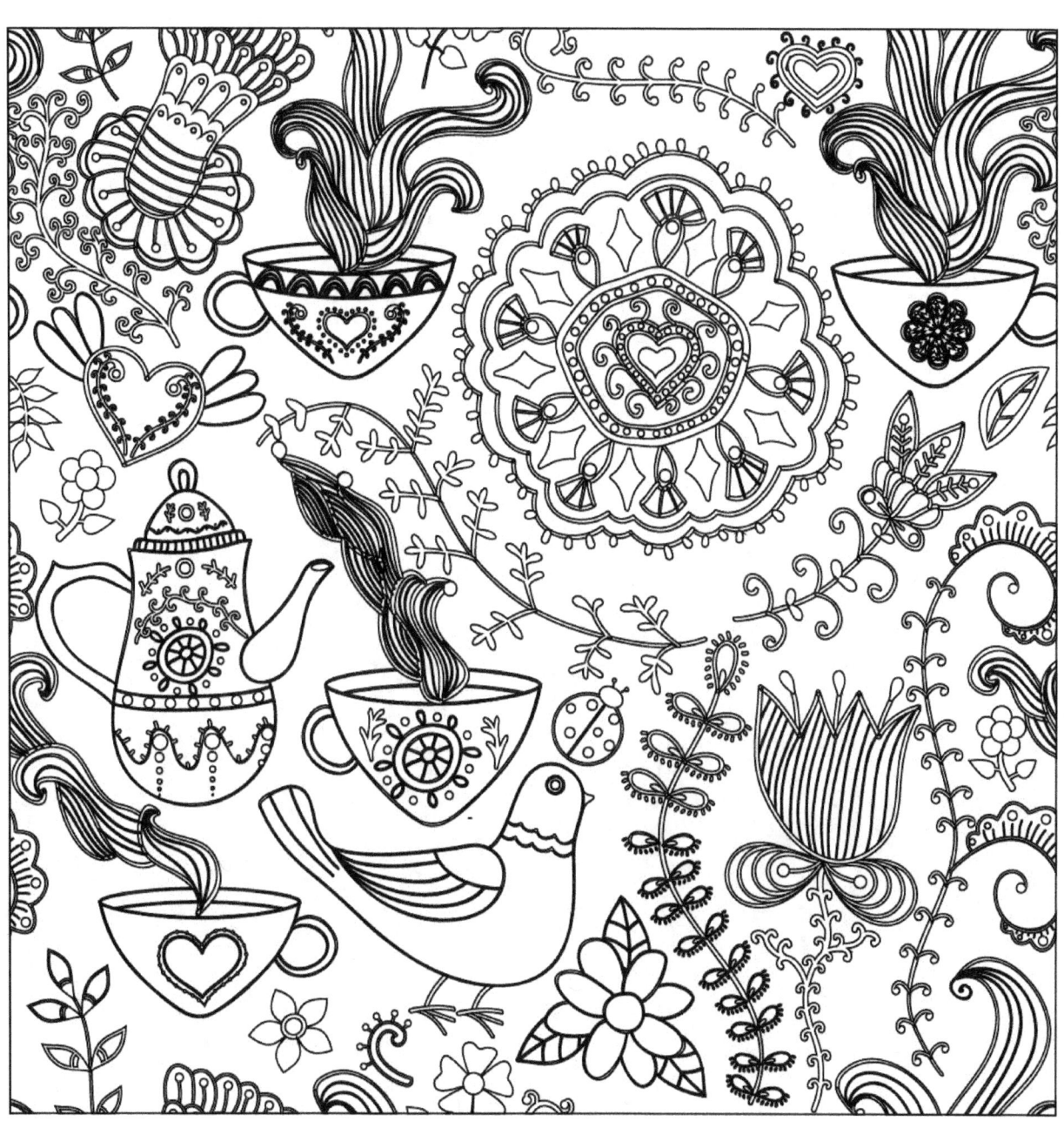

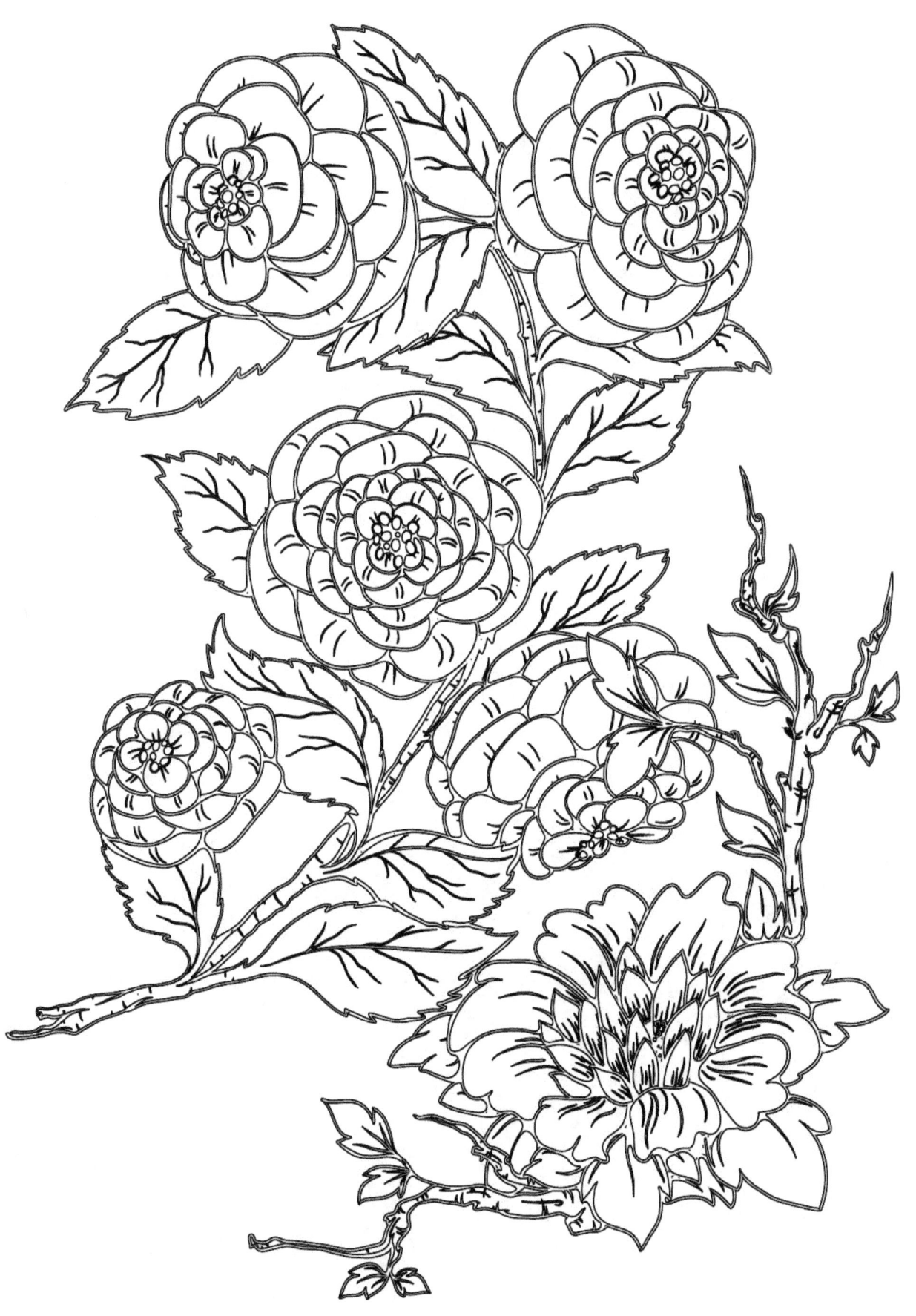

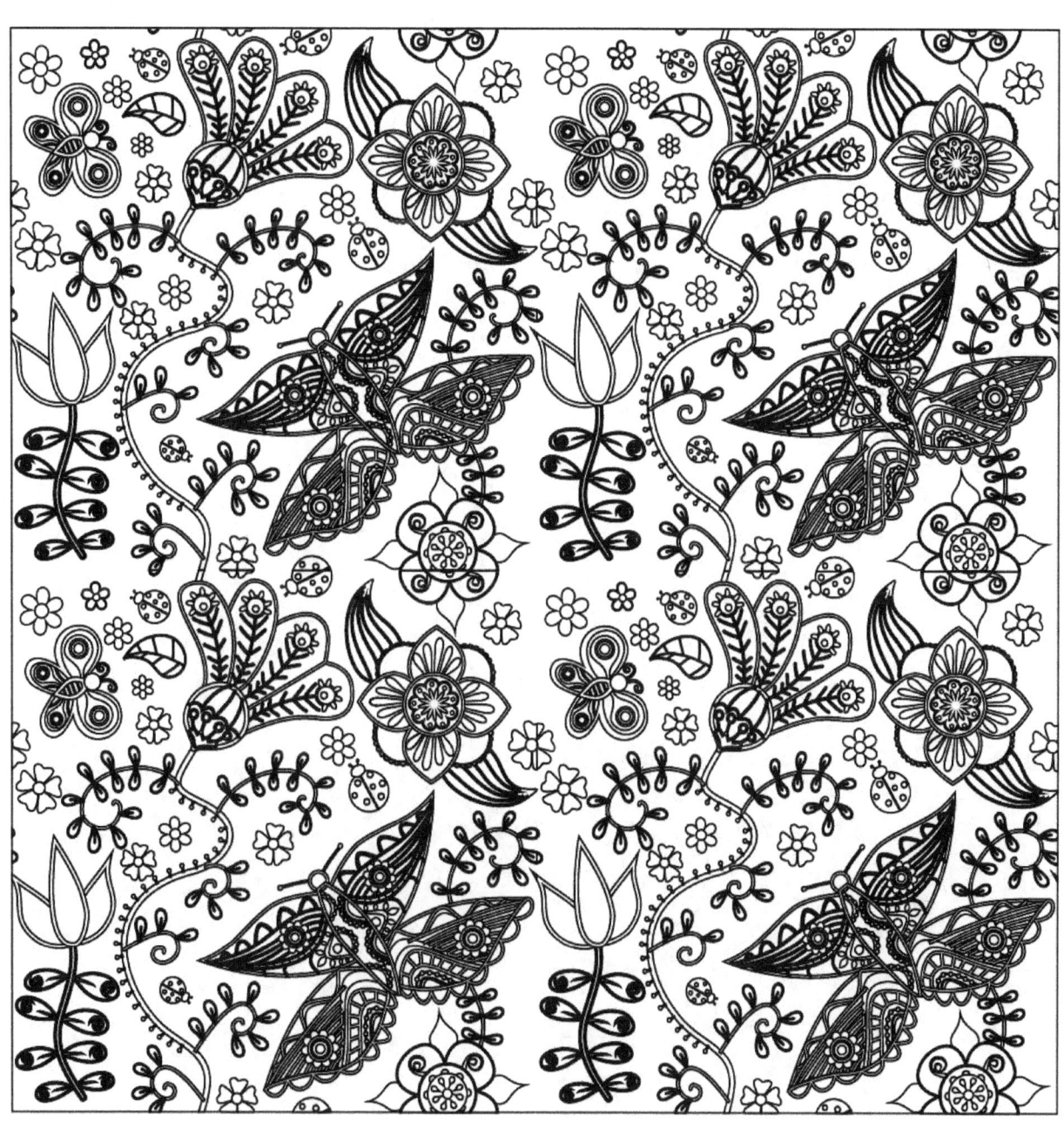

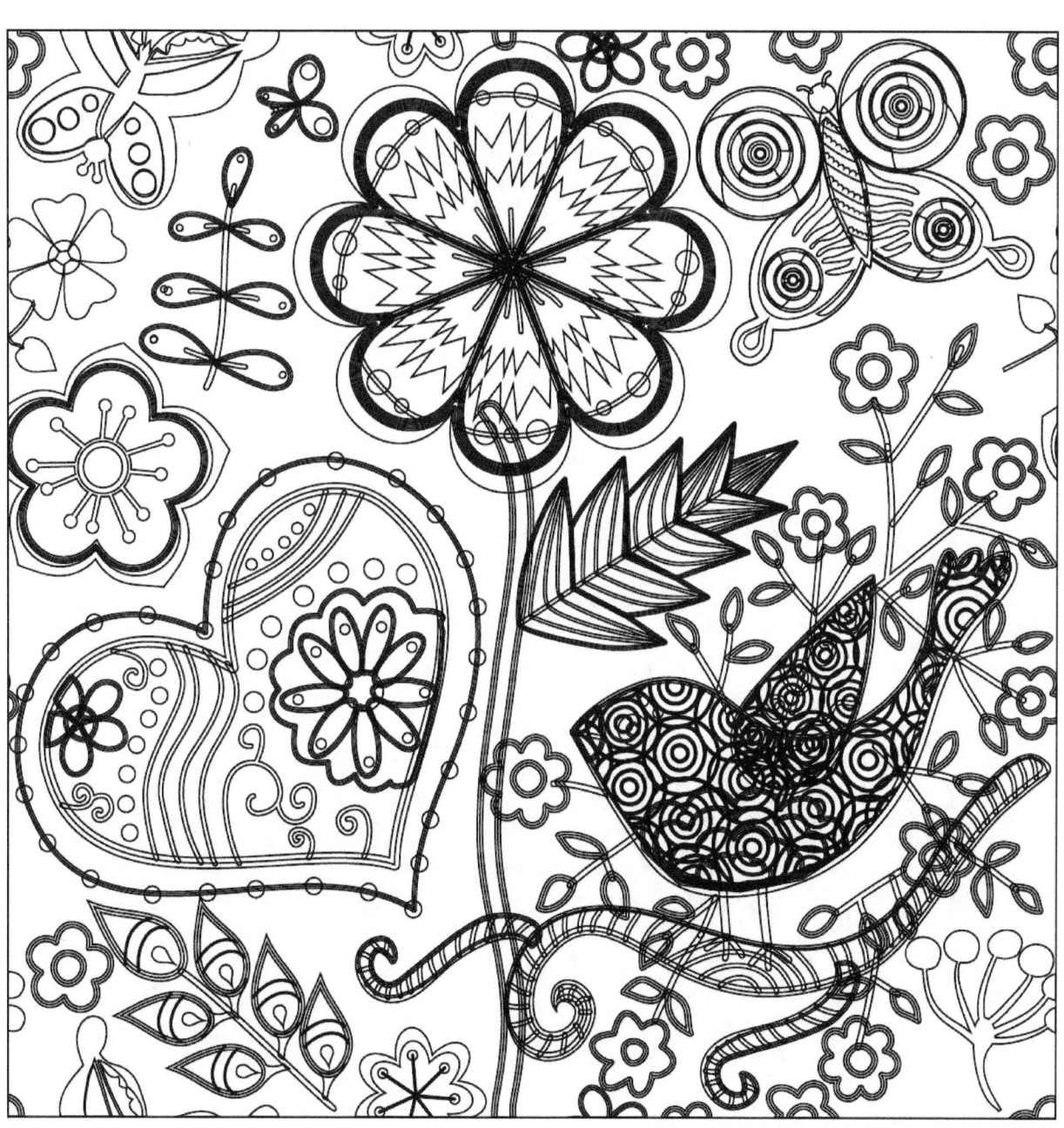

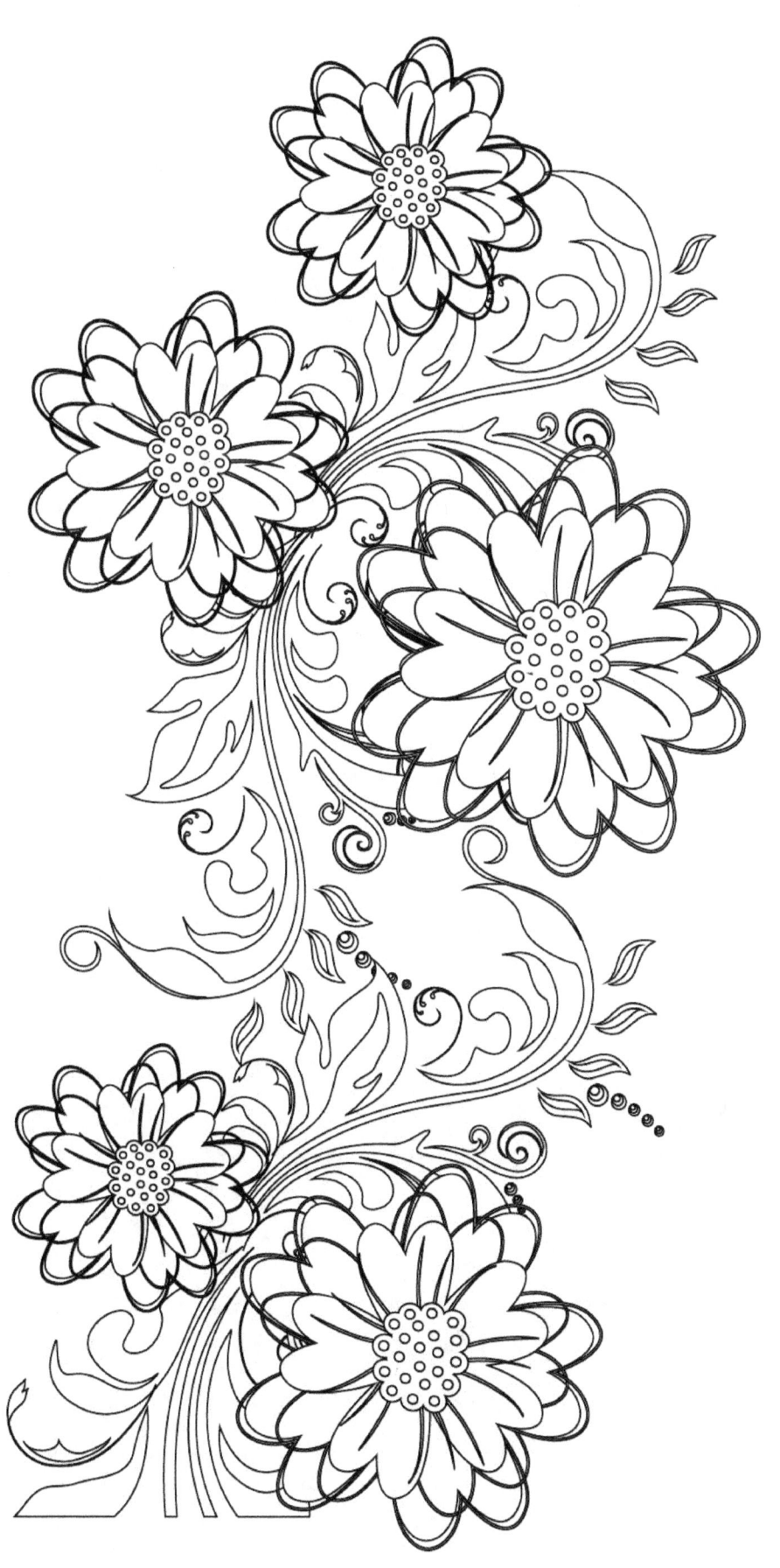

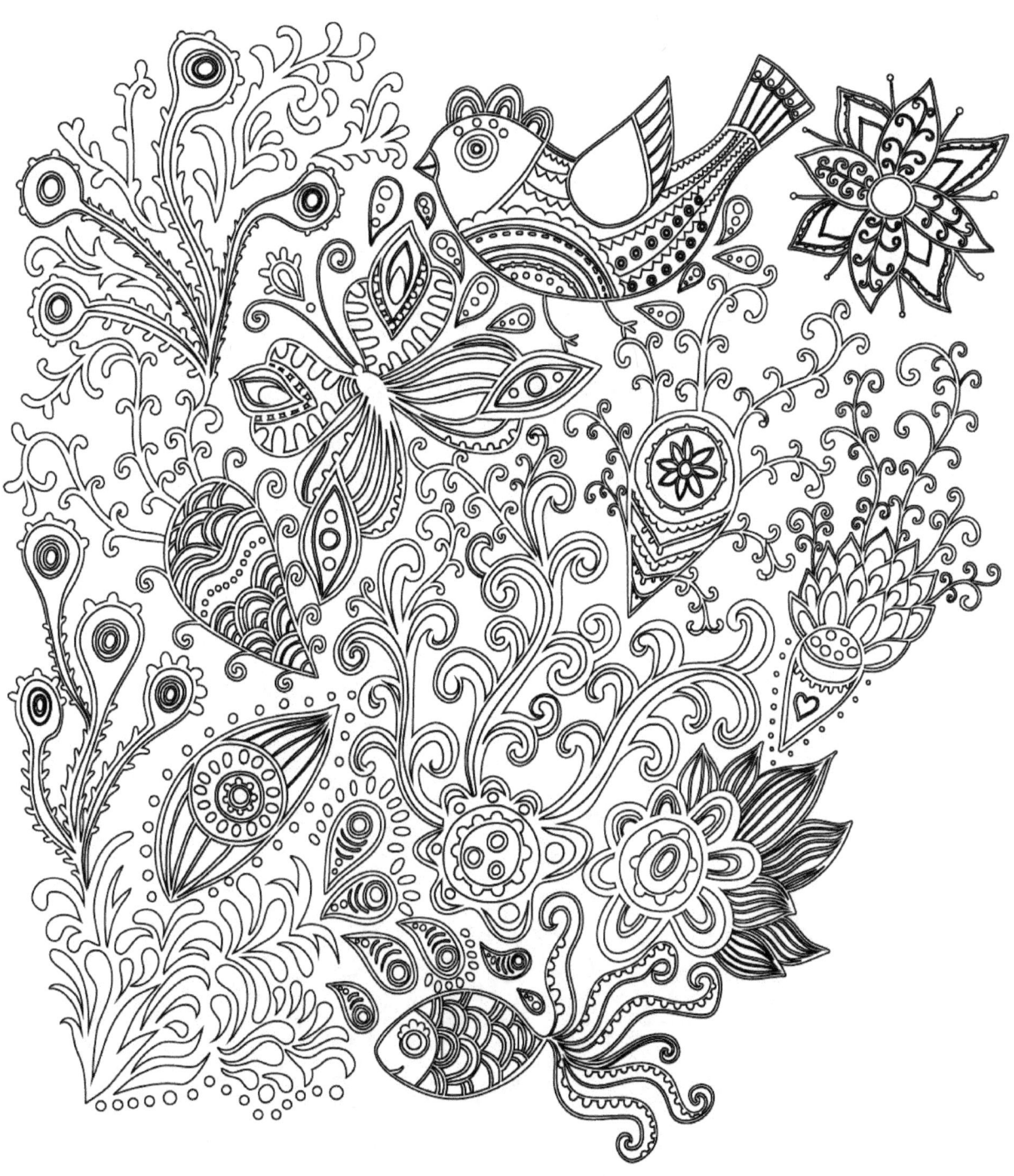

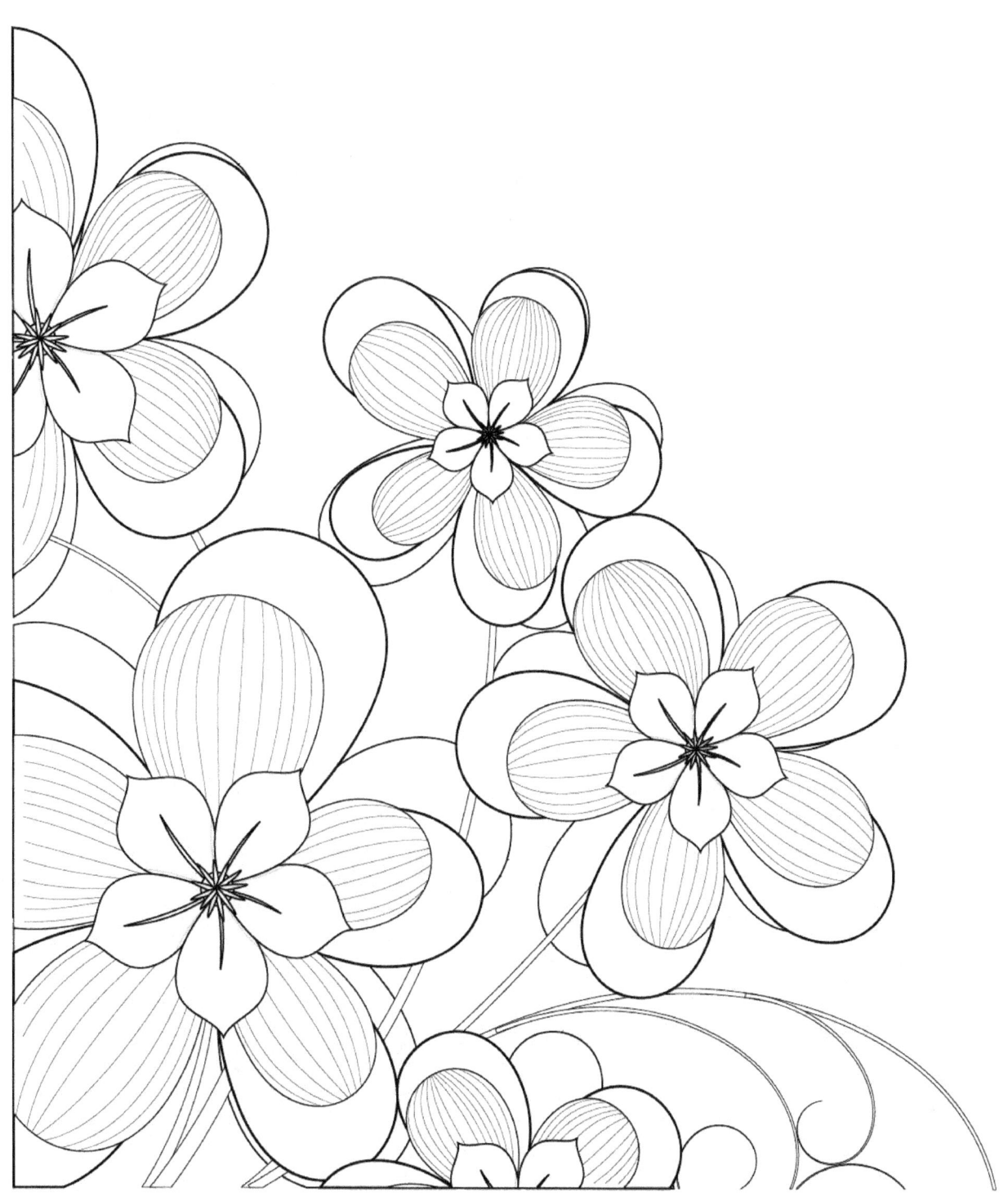

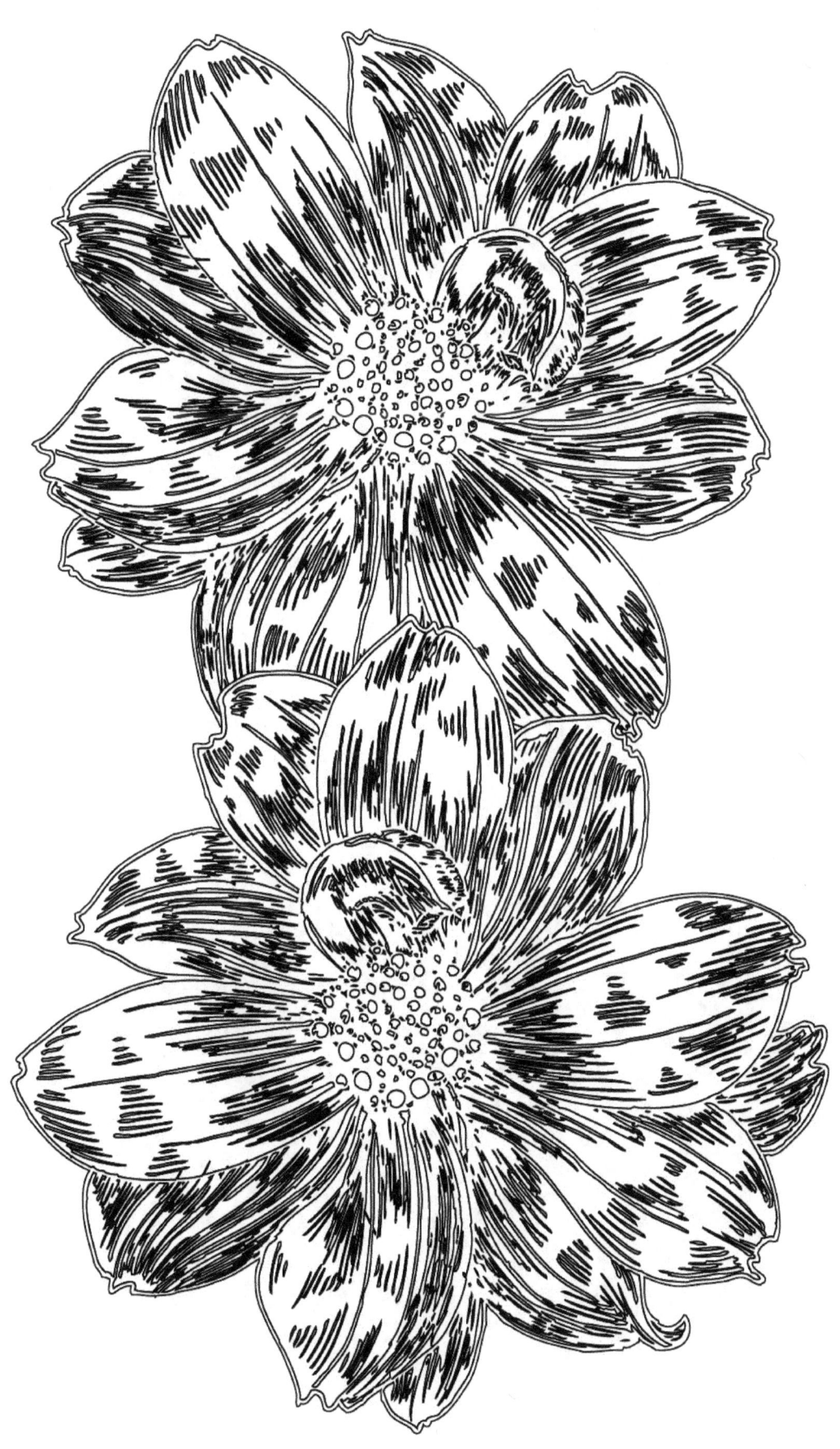

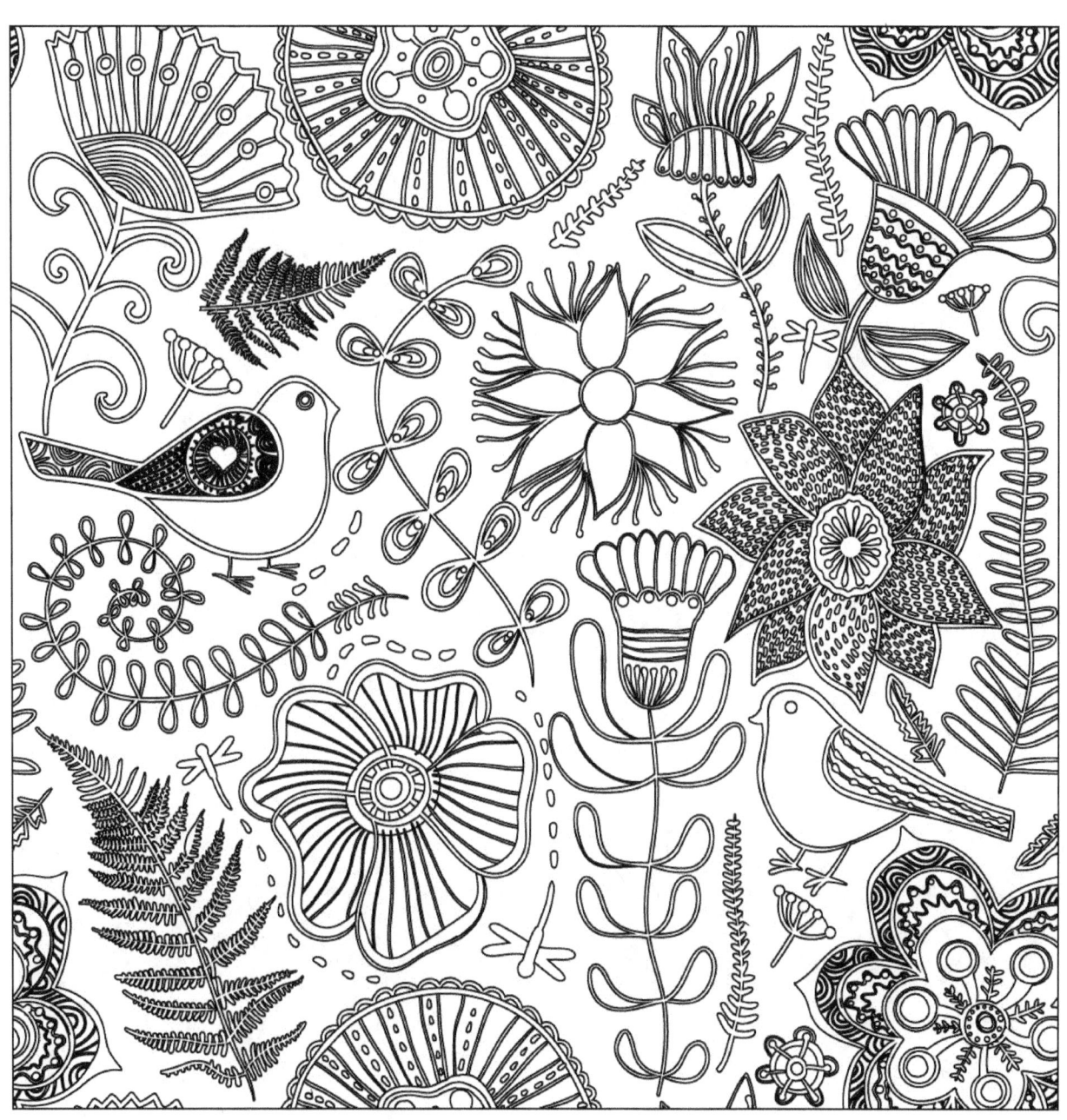

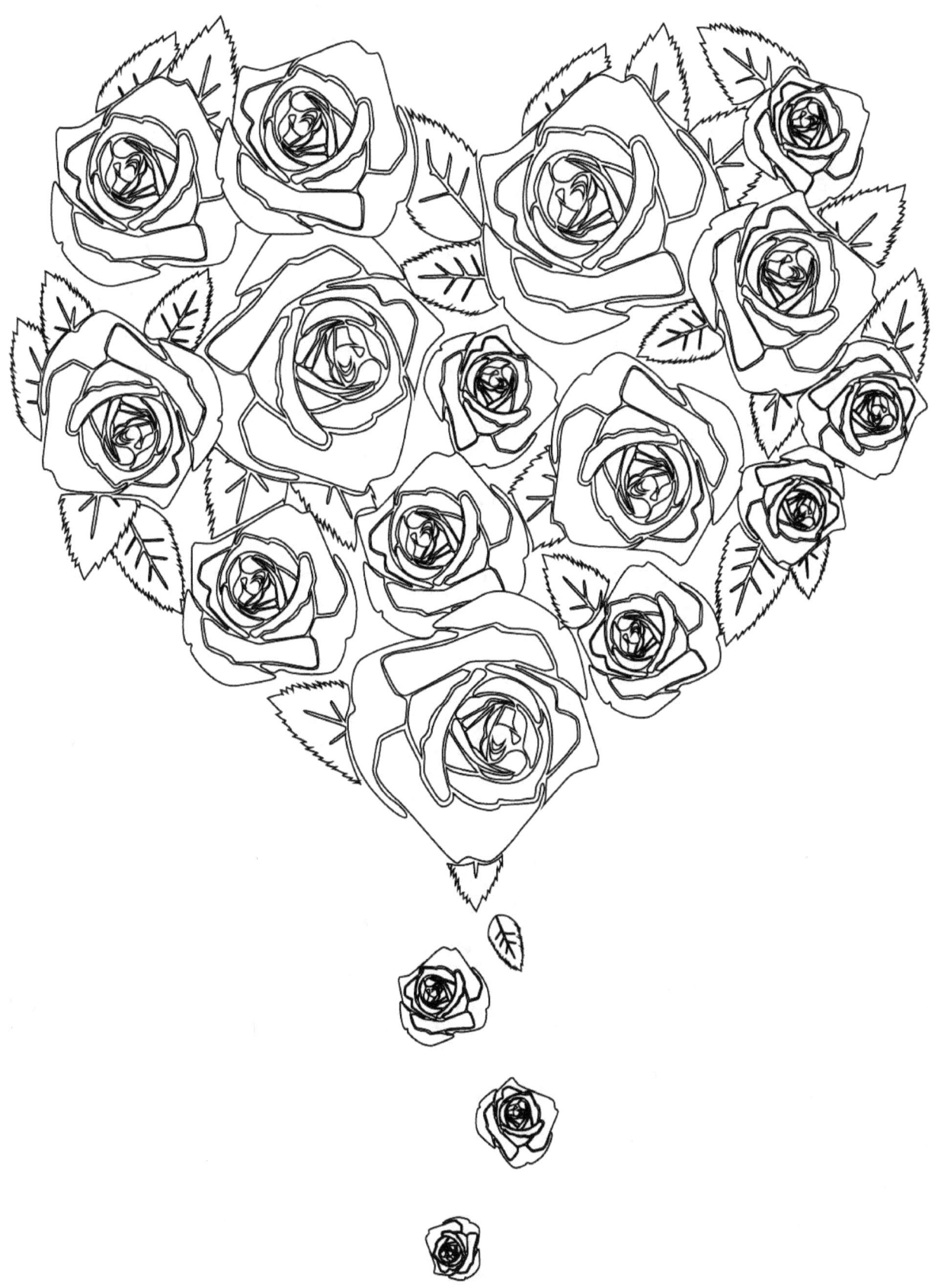

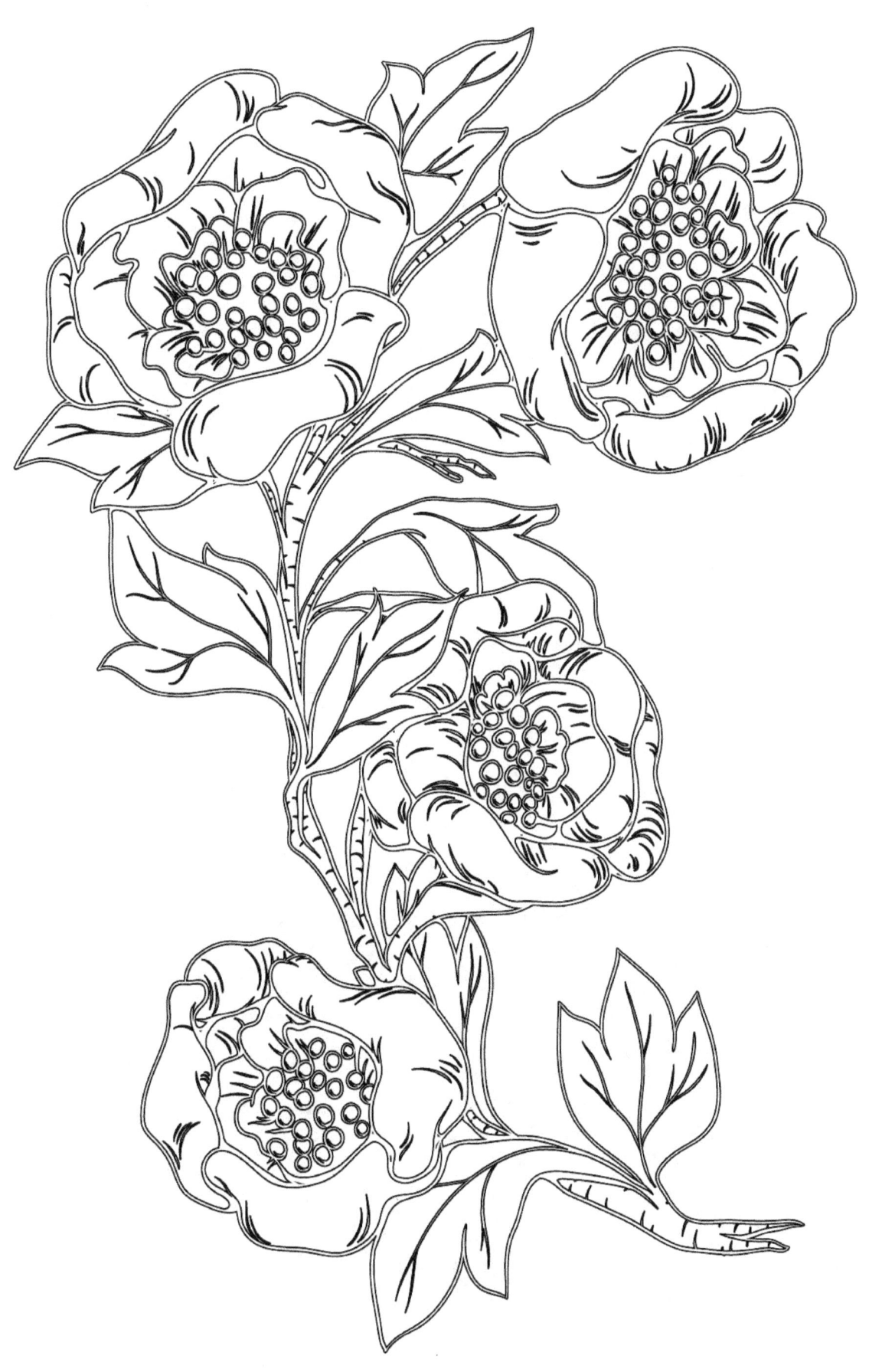

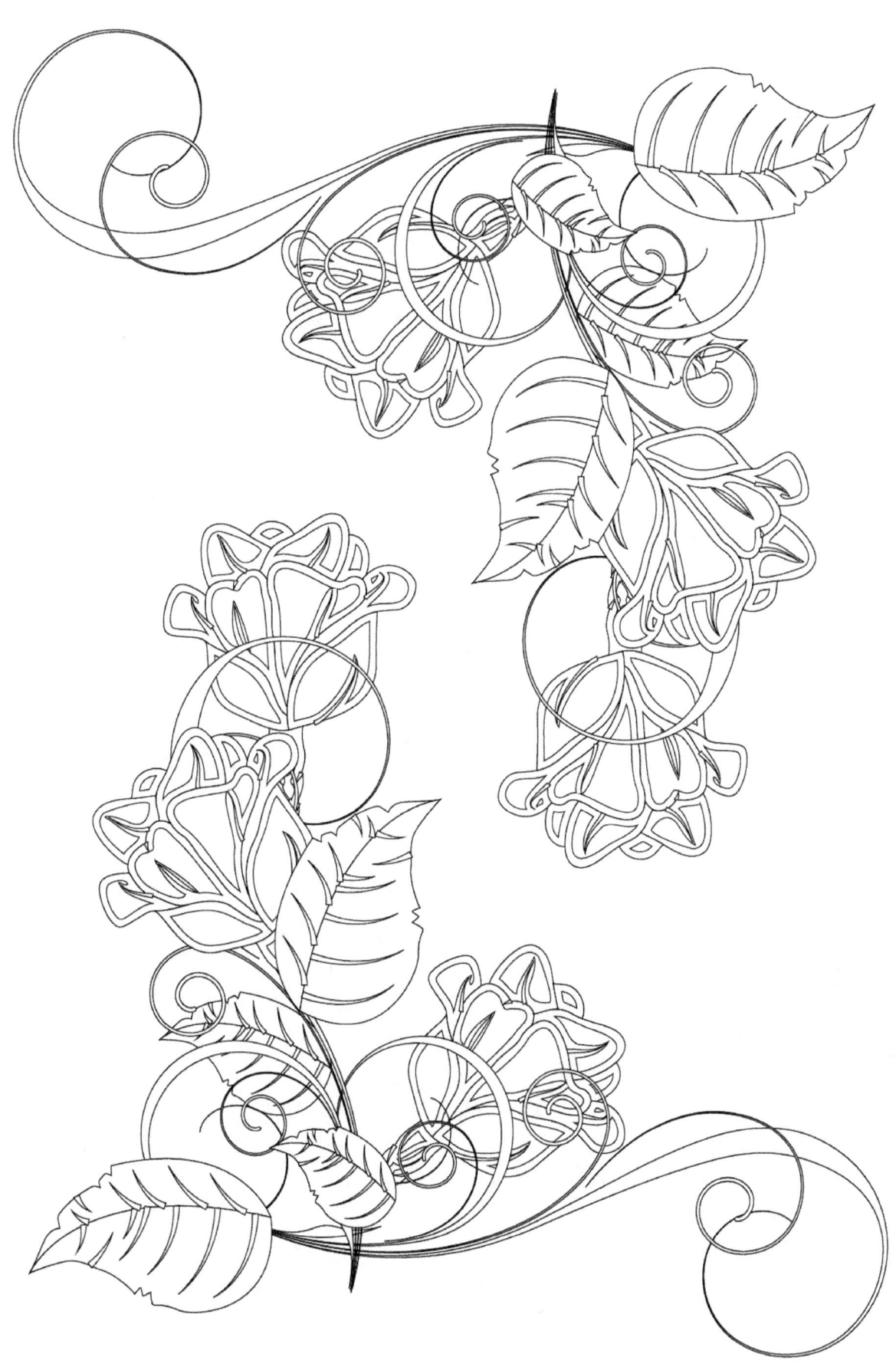

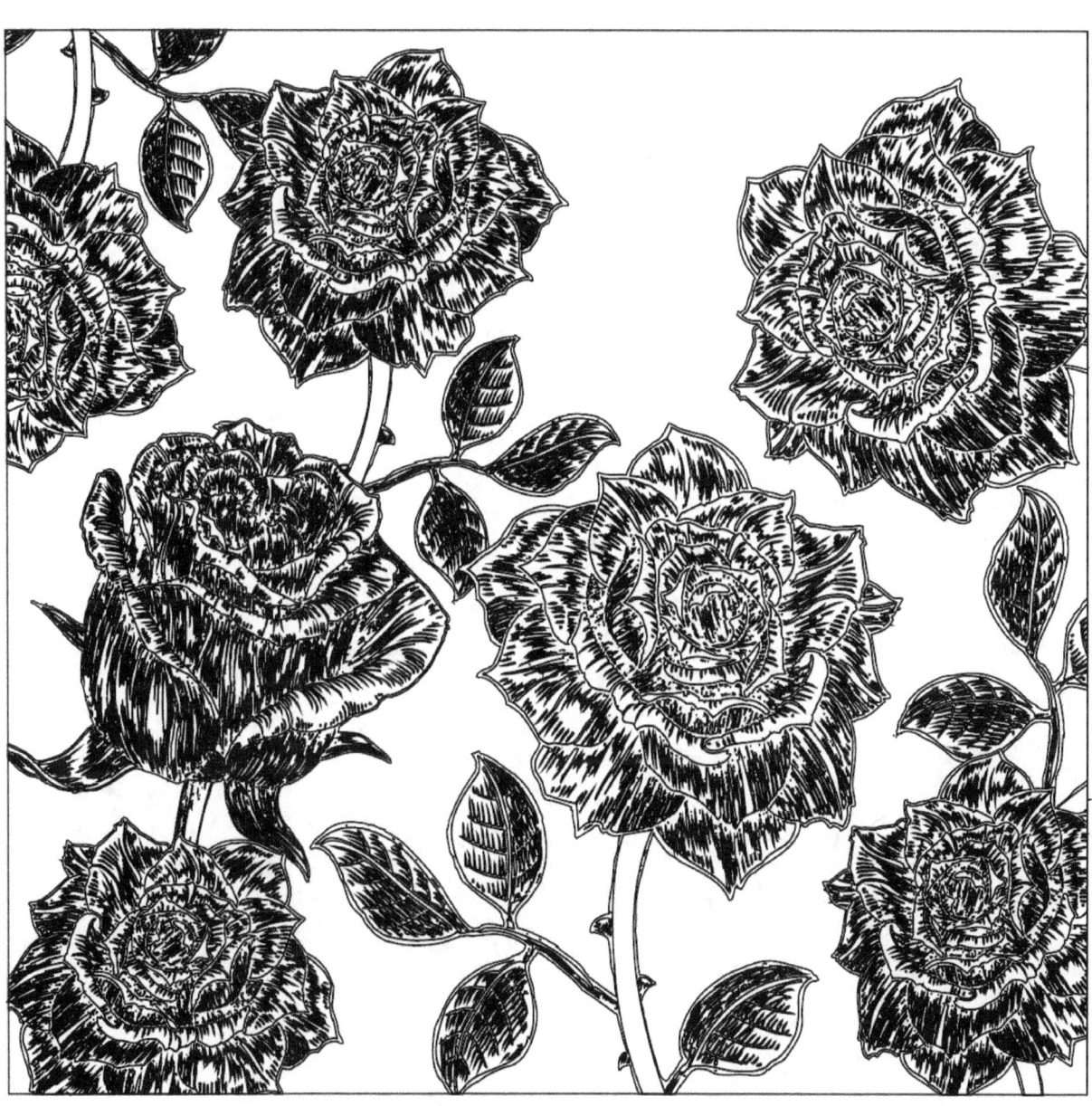

www.ingramcontent.com/pod-product-compliance
Lightning Source LLC
Chambersburg PA
CBHW052016280526

45793CB00005B/1009